BETRAYA

MW01600939

A Memoir-Inspired Journey of Healing, Discernment, and
Spiritual Justice

By Nightingale

Copyright

© Nightingale. All rights reserved. This work is presented for inspirational and educational purposes.

Dedication

To every soul who trusted too easily, loved too deeply, and learned wisdom through pain. May your light remain unbroken.

Foreword

This book was born from lived experience — a life of giving, loyalty, and faith tested by betrayal, jealousy, and the quiet politics that flourish behind polite smiles.

You hold a work that is both testimony and toolkit: poems to open the heart, narratives to name the truth, and reflections to guide your next steps. It is written as a memoir in spirit, safely crafted without naming or accusing any real person.

If you have ever felt misunderstood, mistreated, or overlooked — take courage. Truth moves on God's timeline. Until then, may these pages steady your spirit, sharpen your discernment, and remind you that your worth was never in question.

Acknowledgments

To the quiet supporters who believed in me when I could barely believe in myself; to the mentors who taught me boundaries without bitterness; to the readers who will carry this message forward — thank you.

Above all, to God — who revealed truth in His time and guarded my name when I could not.

Contents

Chapter 1: Innocence in a World of Hidden Motives

Before the Shadows

Before the shadows found me,

my heart walked unguarded—

trusting smiles, believing words,

seeing the world through unbroken glass.

Before the shadows found me,

I carried joy the way others carried fear,

never knowing that light draws envy,

and purity invites tests.

Before the shadows found me,

I believed goodness lived in everyone,

and that harm only came from strangers.

I did not yet understand

that betrayal wears familiar faces.

Yet even after the shadows came,

my light lived on—

because I was born from truth,

not from the darkness that tried to shape me.

Some people are born into stability. Others are born into responsibility.

I was the second kind.
From a young age, I carried more than any child should — not because I wanted to, but because life placed those roles in my hands. While other children were learning games, I was learning sacrifice. While they were running freely, I was helping raise younger children, comforting adults in distress, and stepping into duties far beyond my years.

But those early burdens did something unexpected to me: they made me compassionate instead of cold, open instead of guarded, soft instead of hardened. I believed that if I poured goodness into the world, the world would return it. I believed people meant what they said. I believed sincerity was universal.

In the workplace, I entered with that same openness. I mistook friendliness for sincerity and position for character. I dismissed early red flags — strange tones, forced smiles, compliments with no warmth. Innocence has a blind spot, and blind spots are where betrayal begins.

This chapter is the moment innocence first met reality: the moment trust met caution. And yet, even as innocence faded, something stronger emerged — discernment, wisdom, awareness, strength.

Reflection Questions

• What part of your childhood shaped the way you trust others today?

• Have you ever ignored early signs of someone's harmful intentions?

• Which traits from your innocence do you still value today?

• What strengths were born from the challenges you faced early in life?

Chapter 2: The Workplace Mask

The Mask They Wore
They smiled with practiced ease,

voices sweet as borrowed honey.

But beneath the sugar-coated tone,

a quiet envy stirred.

Masks painted with friendship,

eyes shadowed with unspoken motives—

I did not yet know

that masks can mimic loyalty,

and shadows can follow light.

Workplaces are stages where everyone wears a role. I believed every face was genuine. At first, everything seemed warm: compliments, laughter, and the word dependable attached to my name. But warmth can be misleading when it comes from people who wear emotions like costumes.

Subtle signs appeared: whispers that stopped when I entered, questions that felt like tests, public praise paired with private distance. The mask slipped when my success began to show; jealousy often wears the smile of false concern.

As I kept working with integrity, the masks cracked — through small betrayals disguised as misunderstandings, through exclusions and withheld information. No matter how beautiful the mask, time revealed the face behind it.

Reflection Questions

• Have you ever misjudged someone as genuine when their intentions were not pure?

• What signs now help you distinguish sincerity from pretense?

• How do you respond when someone's mask begins to slip?

• What workplace behaviors have taught you the most about hidden motives?

Chapter 3: When Loyalty Meets Cruelty

The Weight of Giving

I gave without measure—

from a heart unguarded,

from a spirit that believed

loyalty was a universal language.

But cruelty speaks in whispers,

in silent betrayals,

in truths twisted by jealous tongues.

Still, even as loyalty met cruelty,

I learned this truth:

A heart that loves deeply

cannot be dimmed by those

who fear its light.

I lived with loyalty as my compass, believing devotion would be honored. But loyalty is often misunderstood by those who have never truly practiced it. Some interpret giving as a resource to exploit. The cruelty arrived in quiet waves: jokes with edges, shifting tones, and whispers.

The harsh truth: loyalty cannot shield you from those who mistake kindness for weakness. The deepest pain came from those I trusted most. In the breaking, I learned that loyalty to others should never outweigh loyalty to myself. Cruelty taught me discernment, boundaries, and protection of what once lay exposed.

Reflection Questions

• When has loyalty blinded you to someone's true intentions?

• What signs of cruelty did you overlook in the past, and why?

• How do you now differentiate between those who deserve your loyalty and those who do not?

• What boundaries have you developed to protect your heart moving forward?

Chapter 4: The Sting of Envy

When Eyes Turn Green

Envy has a quiet hunger,

a bitterness wrapped in silk.

It watches your steps,

counts your blessings,

measures your light

against its own shadows.

It smiles with tight lips,

praises with hollow words,

and hopes your shine will dim—

failing to realize

that true light

cannot be stolen.

Envy rarely announces itself. It hides behind laughter, compliments, even concern. In the workplace it became a shadow following my achievements. People who once praised my work began to diminish it; small victories became points of tension.

Envy reveals more about the person who carries it than the one they target: insecurity, fear, unhealed wounds. Understanding that truth softened the blow — but understanding does not excuse behavior. Envy taught me to celebrate myself, stand firm in my strengths, and walk away from those threatened by my light.

Reflection Questions

• When have you experienced envy directed toward you, and how did it reveal itself?

• How do you currently respond when others seem threatened by your growth?

• What have you learned about maintaining confidence where envy exists?

• How do you differentiate between genuine support and hidden resentment?

Chapter 5: Lessons in Discernment

Eyes That Finally See

I used to greet the world

with open palms and open doors.

But now my spirit knows:

not every knock deserves an answer,

not every smile deserves a place in the heart.

Discernment is the quiet wisdom

that protects the light within.

Discernment is born from experience. I learned to listen to energy, not words. Access to my life is a privilege, not a right. Silence is an answer when patterns speak for themselves. Promises are easy; consistency is rare.

Not every battle needs my response, not every rumor my correction. Most importantly, I am responsible for my peace. I cannot control others' intentions, but I can control who I allow into my heart, my energy, and my life.

Reflection Questions

• What has life taught you about trusting energy over words?

• What boundaries have you recently placed to protect your peace?

• How do you identify when behavior no longer aligns with promises?

- Where do you need stronger discernment right now?

Chapter 6: Surviving the Storm

The Storm That Could Not Break Me

The winds rose fierce,

the clouds turned dark,

and every whisper became a weapon.

But even in the storm's roar,

my spirit refused to fold.

For storms do not break

what God Himself has strengthened.

They only reveal the strength

that was hidden until the rain fell.

Storms arrive without warning. Mine was built from whispers, shifting glances, and betrayals dressed as misunderstandings. The people I believed would stand with me stepped away. For a time, the storm felt overpowering — confidence wavered, trust shattered.

But I remembered: I had survived worse. Each attack strengthened me; each lie pushed me closer to truth; each betrayal sharpened my discernment. Storms do not destroy the strong; they remind the strong who they are. In surviving, I discovered my greatest truth: I am unbreakable.

Reflection Questions
• What storm forced you to discover your inner strength?

- Who revealed their true character during your hardest moments?

- How do you protect your peace when chaos surrounds you?

- What truth did you uncover after surviving your storm?

Chapter 7: Turning Pain Into Purpose

From Wounds to Wings

My pain was once a wound—

deep, breathless, raw.

Now it is a wing,

lifting me toward the woman

I was always meant to be.

For every hurt became a lesson,

and every tear became a seed,

from which purpose blossomed—

undaunted, undeniable, free.

Pain can break us open, but it can also transform us. What once felt like destruction became awakening. I chose to turn pain into wisdom, boundaries, spiritual awareness, and protection for others. Pain did not defeat me; it deepened me. Every heartbreak became a stepping stone, every injustice a teacher, and in that growth I found purpose.

Reflection Questions

• What pain pushed you toward transformation rather than defeat?

• How has past hurt shaped your present wisdom?

• What purpose have you discovered through struggle?

• How can your story uplift and protect others?

Chapter 8: God's Timing and Truth

In His Perfect Time
Truth walks slowly,

but it never walks alone.

It carries God's hand upon it,

steady, unwavering, sure.

While lies sprint ahead,

built on fear and trembling steps,

truth moves with purpose—

revealing itself

in God's perfect time,

in God's perfect way.

When we are hurting, we want immediate justice. But God's timing is deliberate. Instead of rushing justice, He allowed me to grow. Instead of exposing others immediately, He revealed character gradually. Instead of defending me in front of others, He strengthened me within.

Truth does not need an audience to exist; it exists because God is truth. When truth finally reveals itself, it needs no argument — only recognition. In God's timing, truth both vindicates and transforms.

Reflection Questions

- When has truth revealed itself without your forcing it?

- How has waiting strengthened your faith or character?

- What might God have protected you from by delaying truth?

- How can you practice more trust in God's timing?

Chapter 9: Healing and Rebuilding

The Slow Bloom
Healing is not loud.

It does not demand attention.

It arrives softly—

like morning light creeping over a broken horizon.

It teaches the heart to breathe again,

to trust gently,

to rise without trembling.

And in that quiet rebirth,

we learn that healing

is not returning to who we were—

but becoming who we were meant to be.

Healing is not linear. It bends and pauses and then steps forward with new intention. I had to admit I was hurt and let myself feel it. Rebuilding required patience: relearning to trust my judgment, set boundaries without guilt, and recognize my worth without external validation.

Forgiveness became a release, not a reunion. I chose spaces that value my presence and people who uplift, not drain. Healing did not return me to who I was; it transformed me into someone wiser, stronger, and grounded in truth.

Reflection Questions

- What emotions are you now ready to acknowledge?

- What small signs of healing have you noticed lately?

- Who contributes to your peace — and who disrupts it?

- What does rebuilding look like for your future self?

Chapter 10: Rising Into Your Future

Becoming the Dawn

I am no longer who I was—

shaped by storms,

softened by healing,

strengthened by truth.

I rise now,

not as the wounded,

but as the awakened.

The past is my teacher,

the future is my canvas—

and I am becoming the dawn

I once prayed for.

This is the moment of rising — not returning to what was, but stepping boldly into what can be. Rising means letting go of weights, releasing guilt for walking away from misaligned people, embracing opportunities without fear, and trusting the wisdom I fought to earn.

My future is shaped not by others' opinions but by my resilience and courage. The past prepared me; the lessons equipped me; my spirit aligned with something greater. This rise is powerful — and it is only the beginning.

Reflection Questions

• What vision do you hold for your future now that you have healed?

• What habits or connections must you release to rise fully?

• How will you nurture your growth in this new chapter?

• What does stepping boldly into your future mean for you emotionally and spiritually?

About the Author

Nightingale is a pen name chosen to honor the voice that survived darkness and learned to sing again. Rooted in faith and resilience, Nightingale writes about discernment, healing, and spiritual justice — offering practical wisdom for people navigating betrayal and toxic environments.

Back Cover Summary (Reference Copy)

Betrayal of Trust is a memoir-inspired guide for anyone who has been wounded by lies, envy, or hidden agendas. Through luminous poems, honest storytelling, and reflective questions, Nightingale charts a path from shock to clarity, from pain to purpose, and from fear to faith. Inside you will learn how to: Recognize masks and hidden motives without losing your compassion; Guard your spirit with wise boundaries and quiet confidence; Turn pain into purpose that protects others; Trust God's timing as truth reveals itself. Your light was never the problem — you simply needed discernment to protect it.

Made in the USA
Middletown, DE
24 February 2026

29056332R00019